Networking Struggles?

Don Barnes

Published by Don Barnes, 2024.

LifeWorksInThrees.com

Table of Contents

About the Author

Don is the founder and author of Life Works in Threes!™ E-books. He is a lifelong Texan who has traveled extensively while taking a keen interest in human behavior. His curiosity about life and what drives humans led him to the discovery of how life works in threes. He coined this term as the *Tryune Concept*.

Don attended college on an athletic scholarship and then embarked on a 30-year career in the oil and gas industry. Since the year 2000, he has been a consultant for distributors and manufacturers of various industries. Along the way, he worked on his Tryune discovery in hopes of someday sharing his findings with those struggling unnecessarily... in life. What Don surmised from 40+ years of R&D was that people were struggling unnecessarily because they were not aware that "life works in threes." They, for the most part, have been living their lives <u>by chance</u> rather than <u>by choice,</u> he also discovered.

From this, he began focusing on the "mechanics of life" which shows formulas for success with subjects such as *life, health, money, purpose and so forth*. When people are able to grasp the Tryune Concept, they can apply the formulas with topics that interest them and begin eliminating the struggle. This epiphany is what triggered his Tryune venture and is now on the path of sharing with all who desire to improve on their lives.

Don currently resides in Southern California and Texas while overseeing his businesses and investments.

Life Works in Threes™

When I was a kid growing up, no one sat me down and said, "Okay Don, I'm going to show you how life works so that you can navigate your way through adulthood." I graduated from school, got married and went about my way with the "learn as you go" concept. It was kind of like putting together a backyard swing set without a set of instructions. Lots of frustration and do-overs, for sure!

My discovery of the "triune" word and noticing how things come together in threes is really what set me off on researching that maybe "life comes in three" ...sort of a mechanical approach to managing life, if you will. I combed the libraries and bookstores for information on this and found one book on the subject that was written back in 1951. The author's name was John S. Arant.

What Mr. Arant had to say is this "For lack of a better name, I have called this *The Triangle of Triumph* and therefore, consistent with the name, since most of these conclusions are built on the geometric figure of the triangle." He continued "All Life and all lives are seated in, and circumscribed by, the triangle. The Author and Source and Director of all life is Himself triune in character – Father, Son, and Holy Spirit. Man is of triple nature – body, mind, and spirit – and within those three there are many triangles – desires, development, decay; intellect, will, sensibilities. Of this "paced interlude in the midst of eternity" which we call time there is the triangle of Past, Present, and Future. Space – that limitless and measureless element of the physical universe – is best known in terms of Height, Breadth, and Depth. Try building yourself some triangles along the lines of your Will, your Work, your Way – You will find some interesting angles.

So, for the first time, I realized that life is designed in a mechanical way to come in threes. That means you don't have to rely on wishing and hoping things turn out okay. You can actually look at the three parts that a particular thing is made of and then apply them to get what you're wanting. Like a three-ingredient recipe or a combination lock. With a combination lock, you need the three exact numbers to unlock the lock...otherwise you will continue to struggle.

Some 40 years later, I accumulated things that work in threes and that's when I knew I needed to share this with anyone wanting answers. To have success/harmony in your life, just apply the three parts of an area you're working on, and things will fall into place. I also learned that the recipe for success with just about anything is by doing these three things, consistently – THINK positively, SPEAK positively and ACT positively. For example, if I want to be a successful artist. I would think to myself "I can do this because I have the talent." Then I would speak it this way "Yes, I am working on my art degree and plan to do portraits professionally." Finally, I would act on that by taking art classes and continue crafting my skill. Eventually, I will see the positive results/ success I'm looking for.

Conversely, if I think positively but speak negatively...it will cancel out. Or if I speak positively but have no positive action going on...nothing will happen.

I looked up "How Life Works" and "The Mechanics of Life" and these are really talking about the biology of how our cells work and other chemistry. TRYUNE WORKS! teaches that life is kind of like building blocks. Pick a topic you may be struggling with. See the three parts that topic consists of and then start applying them...on a consistent basis. That will help you overcome the struggle and get you back in harmony/ success with how life works.

For 30+ years I was a golf instructor (by accident). My two kids had some success playing junior golf and so friends and neighbors would ask me to show them and their kids how to play golf successfully. From all of this, I got pretty good at watching golfers on the driving range and could spot right away why they were struggling with hitting bad golf shots. I was able to do that because I knew the three steps to hitting good golf shots. I learned them from studying golf and played for several decades. I "broke the code" for me so to speak.

So now you know that life works in threes. You can live your life *by choice* rather than *by chance* and that my friend… is the key to a fulfilling life.

Introduction

Networking in business is like building a web of connections that can catapult your career or business to new heights. It's not just about collecting business cards or LinkedIn connections; it's about cultivating meaningful relationships that can open doors you didn't even know existed. Imagine your network as your own personal advisory board, filled with mentors, collaborators, and potential clients who can offer guidance, support, and opportunities. These connections can provide valuable insights, introduce you to key players in your industry, and even lead to collaborations that boost your business's visibility and growth.

One of the greatest perks of networking is the exchange of knowledge and ideas. In today's fast-paced world, staying ahead often means staying informed. Through networking, you can tap into the latest trends, industry developments, and best practices shared by others in your field. Whether it's attending conferences, joining professional groups, or simply having coffee with a colleague, these interactions can spark creativity, inspire innovation, and help you adapt to changes in your industry more effectively.

Beyond the immediate benefits, networking fosters a sense of community and belonging. Building relationships with like-minded professionals not only enhances your professional life but also enriches your personal one. Sharing experiences, celebrating successes, and supporting each other through challenges creates a network of trust and camaraderie that can sustain you through both good times and bad. Ultimately, networking isn't just about expanding your business opportunities—it's about building a community that can empower you and those around you to thrive in the ever-evolving world of business.

LIFE WORKS
IN THREES!

My sanctuary on the Pacific coast

My discovery of the Tryune Concept

Before we dive into networking struggles and how to overcome them, let me share my discovery of the Tryune Concept and how life works in threes. It all began in the summer of 1982.

I grew up with parents who treated everyone with decency and respect. My three older sisters and I were raised in a home that was "middle-class traditional." We lived in modest homes in different small towns, attended school and church on a regular basis and celebrated all the traditional holidays. Eventually we settled during the spring of 1964 in the big city of Houston, Texas. I'll never forget the vastness of the city and hearing sirens from police cars, fire trucks and ambulances on a regular basis. I was excited and scared at the same time.

Once settled in this fast-paced city, I finished my growing-up years with an academic diploma and sweetheart intact. I got a job, bought a car, got married, bought a house and produced two beautiful babies in a span of about 5 years. Talk about having to grow up fast!

Things went from great in my childhood to absolute misery in my young adulthood. I began to struggle with my job because deep down I just hated what I was doing. This problem created a snowball effect because soon after, my weight, my finances, my relationships, my happiness and everything else worth saving was going down the drain. I eventually hit a level of frustration that I had never experienced before and didn't know how to get out of it. My cry for help was for anyone or anything to come to my rescue. I just ran out of solutions for my situation.

This is when my discovery happened.

One night shortly after my meltdown, while sleeping soundly, the word "triune" began to softly pound in my head like a mantra. I woke up a little startled and decided to go look up the word in my favorite dictionary (this was WAY before Google.) The definition said '**triune** (try-une) – 1) a group of three things; united. 2) Being 3 in 1 such as *humans are mental, physical and spiritual.* I scratched my head, got a glass of water and went back to bed.

The next day while driving around town, I began thinking about things that I was taught in my younger years that came in threes. My Boy Scout manual taught that to have **character**, I needed to be *1) physically strong, 2) mentally awake and 3) morally straight.* My high school football coach would say emphatically "If you want to be **a good football player**, you have to be *1) mobile 2) agile and 3) hostile*!" My first sales manager shared with me that to be **a successful salesman**, I needed to have *1) sales skills, 2) product knowledge and 3) a good image.*

"Hmm", I thought, "wonder if there are other examples out there of things that work in threes?" So, some 40 years later, I have researched and discovered that many, many things work in threes. What this message was telling me is that to achieve success or balance in any significant area of my life, the three things that area consisted of had to be present continuously. That's when I had my epiphany. This discovery was telling me the secret to how life <u>really</u> works.

Tryune is a play on the word "triune" as an invitation to "try" this concept. Furthermore, we do not say that life <u>only</u> works in threes. Life also works in ones, twos, fours and so on. What has been observed though is that the many things significant to life, just so happen to come and work in threes. That's what is being shared in this book.

Now, you are about to see 40+ years of research and proof that life works in threes. I did not make up any of these topics. I invite you to research them on the internet to validate what is written here. There are some interesting facts that most of us have never realized...until now.

How Life Works in Threes (around 200 examples)

<u>**LIFE**</u>

Humans consist of *body, mind and soul.*

A human's basic needs are *health, income and provisions.*

A human's basic wants are *comfort, gain and approval.*

Our minds are made up of the *conscious, the subconscious and the unconscious.*

Philosophy explains *the id, the ego and superego.*

Atoms consist of *protons, neutrons and electrons.*

Motion is explained by *three basic laws.*

Science falls under three main branches: *natural, social and formal sciences*

Time is *past, present and future...*at the same time.

Electricity consists of *ohms, amperes and voltage.*

Music's basic elements are *duration, pitch and timbre.*

Democracy is a government *of the people, by the people and for the people.*

U.S. branches of government are *the judicial, the executive and the legislative.*

Armed Forces protect us on *land, air and sea.*

Environmentally, we are asked *to reduce, recycle and re-use.*

The news program gives us *the news, sports and conditions.*

Our days consist of *morning, afternoon and evening.*

Three months in each season of the year

Our main meals are known as *breakfast, lunch and dinner.*

A balanced diet consists of *good proteins, carbohydrates and fats.*

Traditional Family consists of *father, mother, and child(ren)*

<u>SCIENCES</u>

Three major branches of natural science – *(physical, earth/ space and life sciences)*

Three major branches of modern physics - *(classical, relativistic, quantum)*

Three major branches of biology *(botany, zoology, microbiology)*

Three spatial dimensions: *height* (up/down), *width* (left/ right) and *depth* (forwards/backwards)

Three-gauge bosons (photon, gluon, W&Z bosons)

Three types of elementary particles *(leptons, quarks, gauge bosons)*

Three quarks in every proton *(two "up" and one "down")*

Three primary colors of light *(red, green, blue)*

Three color tone properties *(hue, value, chroma)*

Three laws of motion (*Newton's laws*)

Three laws of planetary motion (*Kepler's laws*)

Three layers of the Sun's interior (*core, radiative zone, convective zone*)

Three layers of the Sun's atmosphere (*photosphere, chromosphere, corona*)

Three types of meteorites (*iron, stony iron, stony*)

Three types of galaxy shapes (*elliptical, spiral, irregular*)

Three substances of the universe (*normal matter, 'dark matter', 'dark energy'*)

Three phases of the moon (*new moon, first quarter, full moon*)

Three planetary regions (*temperate, sub-tropical, tropical*)

Three layers of the Earth (*crust, mantle, core*)

Three components of an ecosystem (*producers, consumers, decomposers*)

Three types of rocks (*igneous, sedimentary, metamorphic*)

Three types of fossil fuels (*coal, crude oil, natural gas*)

Three hydrological processes (*evaporation, condensation, precipitation*)

Three basic types of (meteorological) precipitation (*liquid, freezing, frozen*)

Three types of substances *(mono-constituent, multi-constituent, UVCB)*

Three phases of (normal) matter *(solid, liquid, gas)*

Three types of covalent chemical bonds *(single, double and triple bonds)*

Three isotopes of hydrogen *(protium, deuterium, tritium)*

Three atoms in each molecule of water *(two hydrogen atoms and an oxygen atom)*

Three endings to salts *(-ide, -ite, -ate)*

Three requirements for fire *(fuel, oxygen, heat)*

Three nucleotide bases in a genetic codon

Three domains of life *(archaea, bacteria and eukaryotes)*

Three major groups of flowering plants *(monocots, eudicots, magnolids)*

Three major functions that are basic to plant growth and development: *(photosynthesis* [making sugars], *respiration* [metabolizing those sugars], and *transpiration* [water vapor loss]

Three things that the chlorophyll in plants needs for photosynthesis to take place: *(sunlight, carbon dioxide and water)*

Transpiration serves three roles: *(cooling the plant, moving minerals* and *sugars through the plant,* and *maintaining the turgidity pressure* [stiffness] *of the plant's cells)*

Three parts of an insect's body *(head, thorax, abdomen)*

<u>BIOLOGY</u>

Three types of cones in the retina, relating to the three primary colors

Three semi-circular canals in the ear *(lateral, anterior, posterior)*

Three sections in the ear *(outer, middle, inner)*

Three ossicles in the middle ear *(malleus, incus, stapes)*

Three segments to each limb *(proximal, mid, distal)*

Three bones in each arm *(humerus, radius, ulna)*

Three joints in the arm *(shoulder, elbow, wrist)*

Three joints in the leg *(hip, knee, ankle)*

Three joints in the elbow *(humeroulnar, humeroradial, proximal radioulnar)*

Three functional compartments in the knee joint *(the femoropatellar, medial femorotibial* and *lateral femorotibial articulations)*

Three types of fibrous joints *(sutures, gomphoses, syndesmoses)*

Three types of bone in each hand (*carpals, metacarpals, phalanges*)

Three types of bone in each foot (*tarsals, metatarsals, phalanges*)

Three bones (phalanges) in each finger and in each toe (*proximal, intermediate, distal*)

Three layers of skin (*dermis, epidermis, hypodermis*)

Three components of a cell (*cell membrane, nucleus, cytoplasm*)

Three types of blood vessels (*arteries, veins, capillaries*)

Three types of blood cells [*red* (erythrocytes), *white* (leukocytes), *platelets* (thrombocytes)]

Three processes of the intestinal tract (*ingestion, digestion, excretion*)

Three germ layers (*Endoderm, Mesoderm, Ectoderm*)

Three parts of a human tooth (*crown, neck, root*)

Three organs of otolaryngology (*ear, nose, throat*)

Three major body systems (*digestive, circulatory, respiratory*)

Three parts to a neuron: (*soma* [*cell body*], *axon, dendrites*)

Three main parts of the brain (*forebrain, midbrain, hindbrain*)

Three parts of the forebrain *(cerebrum, thalamus, hypothalamus)*

Three parts of the midbrain *(colliculi, tegmentum, cerebral peduncles)*

Three parts of the hindbrain *(cerebellum, pons, medulla)*

Three membranes enclosing the brain *(dura mater, arachnoid, pia mater)*

The brain operates on three levels: *consciously* (for cognitive thought and declarative memory); *subconsciously* (for pre-planned actions and procedural memory); and *unconsciously* (for breathing, heart beating, etc.)

Our conscious mind is fed from three sources: *our senses* (which can be fooled); *our memory* (which is flawed); and *our imagination* (which is inventive)

Three aspects of the human mind *(memory, intellect, will)*

Three parts of the human personality *(id, ego, superego)*

The sum of human capacity consists of three abilities *(thought, word and deed)*

Three times of man *(birth, life, death)*

Three periods of the Gait Cycle *(initial double limb support, single limb support, and terminal double limb support)*

MUSIC

Three types of musical notes *(sharps, flats, naturals)*

Three aspects of a song (*lyrics, melody, rhythm*)

Three types of musical chords (*root, third, fifth*)

<u>MATHEMATICS</u>

Three types of a real number (*positive, negative, zero*)

Three parts to any arithmetic operation: for addition: *augend, addend and sum* - for subtraction: *minuend, subtrahend and difference* - for multiplication: *multiplicand, multiplier and product* - for division: *dividend, divisor and quotient*

Three laws of arithmetic operations (*commutative, associative, distributive*)

Three types of equivalence relation (*reflexivity, symmetry, transitivity*)

Three types of symmetry operations (*translation, rotation, reflection*)

Three geometries (*Euclidean, spherical, hyperbolic*)

The number 3 is the basis of an entire branch of mathematics, called trigonometry (from the Greek *trigonon* "triangle" + *metron* "measure")

Three trigonometric functions (*sine, cosine, tangent*)

Three types of average (*mean, mode, median*)

<u>GRAMMAR</u>

Three logical operators (*AND, OR and NOT*)

Three laws of logic (*identity, noncontradiction, excluded middle*)

Three parts of a logical syllogism (*major premise, minor premise, conclusion*)

Three grammatical parts to a sentence (*subject, verb, complement*)

Three persons in grammar [*1st person* (I/we), *2nd* (you or your), *3rd* (he/she/it/they)]

Three genders in grammar [*masculine* (he/him), *feminine* (she/her), *neuter* (it)]

Three forms of comparison in grammar [*positive, comparative* (more, -er), *superlative* (most, -est)]

Three cases in (English) grammar [*subjective/nominative* (he), *objective/accusative* (him) and *possessive/genitive* (his)]

Three parts of a narrative (*beginning, middle, end*)

Components of an essay (*introduction, body, conclusion*)

Elements of a rhetorical appeal (*ethos, pathos, logos*)

Aspects of a story (*plot, characters, setting*)

<u>RELIGION</u>

The Creator – *omniscient, omnipotent, omnipresent*

Christian God – *Father, Son, Holy Spirit*

Jesus – *The Way, The Truth, The Life*

Ancient Near East- *Qudshu, Astarte, Anat*

Classical Antiquity – Many dieties came in threes

Hinduism – Para Brahman is *Brahma, Visnu, Shiva*

Ancient Celtic Cultures – *many example of triad dieties*

Buddhism – *The three jewels*

Taoism – *The three pure ones*

Islam – *Fear, Hope and Love*

Baha'i - *Intention, Power and Action*

Confucianism – *Benevolence, Wisdom and Courage*

<u>OTHER TRIUNE EXAMPLES</u>

3 Coins in a Fountain

3 Days of the Condor

3 Miles in a League

3 Goals in a Hat Trick

3 Piece Suit

3 Feet in a Yard

3 Books in Lord of the Rings

3 Ring Circus

3 Ships of Christopher Columbus

3 Sheets to the Wind

3 Books in a Trilogy

3 Wheels on a Tricycle

3 Wise Men

3-Legged Race

3 Ring Circus

3-Wheeler

3 Cornered Hat

3 Dimensional

3 Musketeers

3 R's (reading, 'riting, 'rithmatic)

3 Sides of a triangle

3 Races in the Triple Crown (horse racing)

3 Angles in a Triangle

3 Trimesters in a Pregnancy

3 Flavors in Neapolitan Ice Cream

3 Stars in Orion's belt

3 Barleycorns in an Inch

3 Hands on a Clock (with the Seconds Hand)

3 Colors in a Flag

3 Minute Egg

3 Great Pyramids at Giza

3 Holes in a Bowling Ball

3 Colors in a Set of Traffic Lights

3 Minutes in a Boxing Round

3 Teaspoons in a Tablespoon

3 Legs on a Stool

3 Monastic Vows (Obience, Stability, Conversatio Morum)

3 Body Types: Endomorph, Mesomorph, Ectomorph

3 Ring Notebooks

3 Germ layers: Endoderm, Mesoderm, Ectoderm

3 Species of Homo: Homo habilis, Homo erectus, Homo sapiens

3 Basic parts of a camera: Lens, Shutter, Sensor

3 Stages of a Project lifecycle: initiation, planning, execution

The Truth, The Whole Truth and Nothing but the Truth

Life, Liberty and the Pursuit of Happiness

Hear no Evil, See no Evil, Speak no Evil

National motto of France/Haiti: Liberty, Equality, Fraternity

Paper, Rock, Scissors

Ready, Aim, Fire

On Your mark, Get Set, Go

Olympic medals of gold, silver, bronze

Types of joints (ball & socket, hinge, pivot)

Stages of a rocket launch (launch, orbit, re-entry)

Parts of a joke (setup, delivery, punchline)

Primary components of a transistor (emitter, base, collector)

Primary components of an airplane (fuselage, wings, empennage)

Basic components of a computer: CPU, memory, storage

Three phases in the development of technology (*eotechnic* [*mechanical*], *paleotechnic* [*steam-powered*] and *neotechnic* [*electric-powered*]

Communication systems require three components (*transmitter, channel, receiver*)

The list goes on. See if you can find more examples as they are everywhere in our universe! Now that you know that life works in threes (with proof!), we can begin to apply this concept to whatever topics we want.

So, to overcome struggles in networking, we need to apply the three areas that networking consists of – BUILD, RECIPROCATE and MAINTAIN. Let's get started!

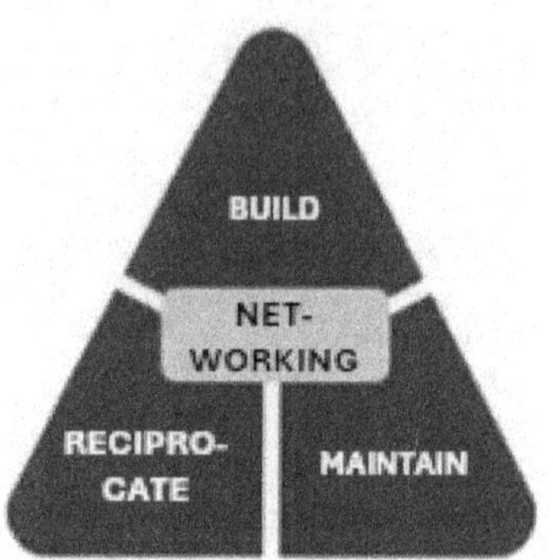
BUILD
NET-
WORKING
RECIPRO-
CATE
MAINTAIN

NETWORKING

Building, reciprocating, and maintaining your network in business is not just beneficial—it's paramount to your success. Imagine your network as a garden: by carefully planting seeds (building relationships), nurturing them with care and attention (reciprocating), and consistently tending to them (maintaining), you ensure a bountiful harvest of opportunities and support. Building your network starts with genuine connections. Whether you're attending industry events, reaching out on social media, or meeting colleagues through mutual acquaintances, each interaction lays the foundation for future collaboration and growth.

Reciprocating within your network is like watering those seeds you've planted. It's about being proactive in offering help, sharing knowledge, and making introductions whenever possible. When you give freely within your network, you create a culture of mutual support and trust. This reciprocity strengthens relationships and encourages others to reciprocate, creating a dynamic where everyone benefits. Whether it's providing advice to a newcomer in your field or recommending a trusted service provider, each act of reciprocity strengthens the fabric of your network.

Maintaining your network is the key to its longevity and effectiveness. Just as a garden requires ongoing care, your professional relationships need nurturing over time. This involves staying in touch regularly, checking in on contacts, and showing genuine interest in their endeavors. Technology makes it easier than ever to maintain connections through social media, email newsletters, or virtual meetups. By staying visible and engaged, you ensure that your network remains vibrant and responsive, ready to support you when needed. Remember, in business and in life, relationships are often the cornerstone of success—cultivating them with care can yield abundant rewards for years to come.

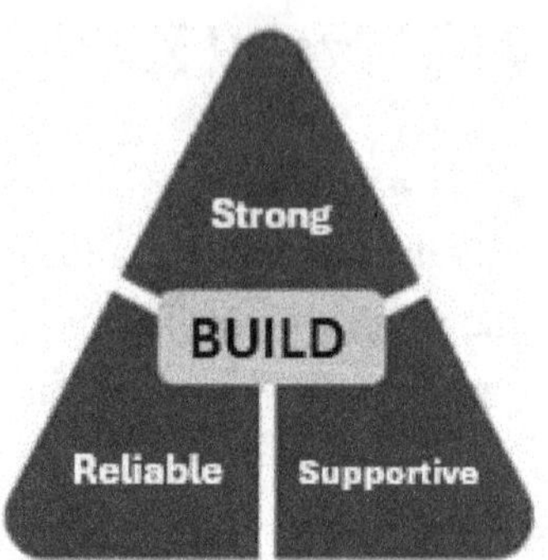
Strong
BUILD
Reliable
Supportive

BUILD

Building your network in business is like laying the foundation for a sturdy house—you want it to be strong, reliable, and supportive. The first key to building your network is a strong list. Be yourself and approach relationships with genuine interest and curiosity. People appreciate sincerity and are more likely to connect with you when they sense authenticity. Whether you're at a networking event or connecting online, focus on building real connections rather than just collecting contacts.

The second key is reliability. Networking isn't a one-time effort; it's about regular engagement and nurturing relationships over time. Stay active in your industry or community by attending events, participating in online discussions, and reaching out to new contacts. Consistency shows your commitment to building meaningful connections and keeps you top of mind when opportunities arise.

Lastly, a supportive network is crucial. Networking is a two-way street, so aim to offer value to others whenever possible. This could mean sharing industry insights, making introductions to helpful contacts, or offering support and advice based on your expertise. When you contribute positively to your network, you not only strengthen existing relationships but also attract new connections who see you as a valuable resource.

By focusing on *strong, reliable, and supportive*, you'll build a network that's not only extensive but also effective in supporting your professional growth and success. Remember, networking is about cultivating relationships that can benefit both parties—approach it with a friendly demeanor and genuine interest in others, and you'll find your network growing naturally over time.

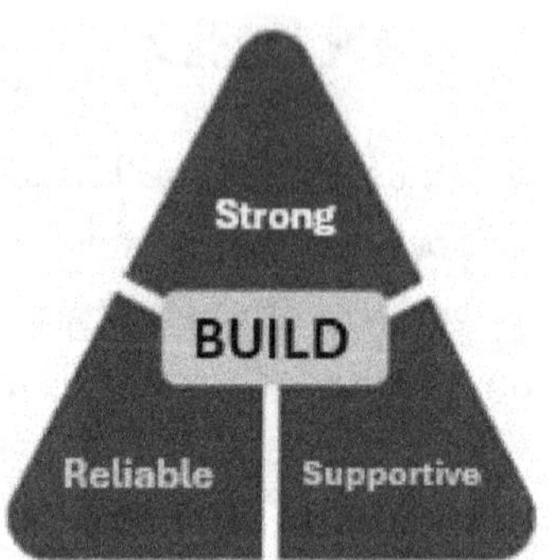
Strong
BUILD
Reliable
Supportive

Strong

Building a strong list of network contacts in business is like assembling your own team of supporters and allies who can help propel your career or business forward. These contacts are more than just names on a list—they represent a diverse range of perspectives, expertise, and opportunities that can enrich your professional journey. Imagine having access to mentors who offer invaluable advice, peers who inspire you with fresh ideas, and clients who trust your capabilities because of a mutual connection. A strong network can open doors to new partnerships, collaborations, and even unexpected career paths.

One of the greatest benefits of a robust network is its ability to provide opportunities for growth and development. Whether you're seeking new clients, exploring career advancement, or looking for guidance on a challenging project, your network can offer insights and connections that might not be available through other channels. Networking isn't just about who you know—it's about who knows you and what you're capable of achieving. By cultivating meaningful relationships with people in your industry or related fields, you create a support system that can help you navigate challenges and seize opportunities with confidence.

Furthermore, building a strong network fosters a sense of community and camaraderie. It's about building relationships based on trust, mutual respect, and a genuine desire to help one another succeed. Through networking events, professional associations, or even social media platforms, you can connect with like-minded individuals who share your passions and goals. These connections not only enhance your professional life but also contribute to your personal growth and well-being. In business, as in life, the strength of your network often determines the breadth of your opportunities and the depth of your impact. So, invest in building and nurturing your network—it's a friendly and rewarding journey that pays dividends in ways you may not expect.

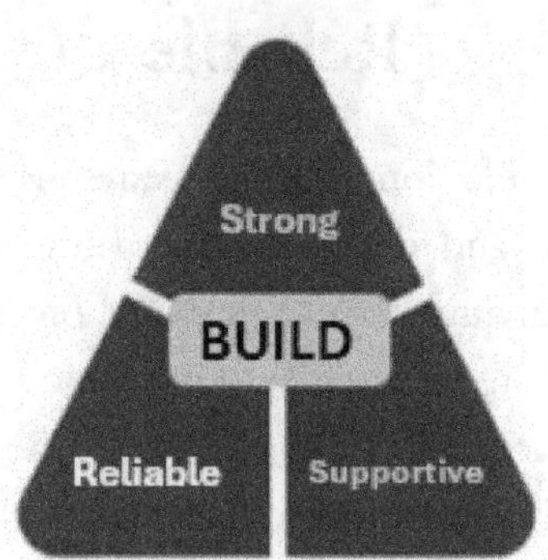
Strong
BUILD
Reliable
Supportive

Reliable

Networking with reliable contacts in business is like building a safety net woven with trust and dependability. These contacts are not just acquaintances but individuals you can count on for support, guidance, and collaboration when needed. In a dynamic business environment, having reliable connections can make all the difference between struggling alone and overcoming challenges with collective strength. Imagine having a circle of trusted advisors who offer sound advice, partners who deliver on their promises, and colleagues who share your commitment to excellence—these relationships form the bedrock of success.

One of the key benefits of networking with reliable contacts is the ability to tap into their expertise and experience. Whether you're navigating a complex project, exploring new markets, or seeking innovative solutions, reliable contacts can provide insights and perspectives that you might not have considered. Their reliability ensures that when they offer assistance or advice, you can trust it to be valuable and constructive. This mutual trust fosters a collaborative spirit where everyone contributes to each other's success.

Moreover, networking with reliable contacts enhances your credibility and reputation within your industry. When you associate yourself with trustworthy individuals who are known for their integrity and professionalism, it reflects positively on your own character and capabilities. This can lead to increased opportunities for partnerships, referrals, and career advancements. By nurturing these relationships over time through consistent communication and genuine interest in their success, you build a network that not only supports you but also elevates your standing in the business community.

In business, reliability is a cornerstone of long-term success. Networking with reliable contacts isn't just about building connections—it's about fostering relationships built on mutual respect, honesty, and shared values. By prioritizing reliability in your network, you create a supportive ecosystem where trust flourishes, opportunities abound, and collective achievements become possible.

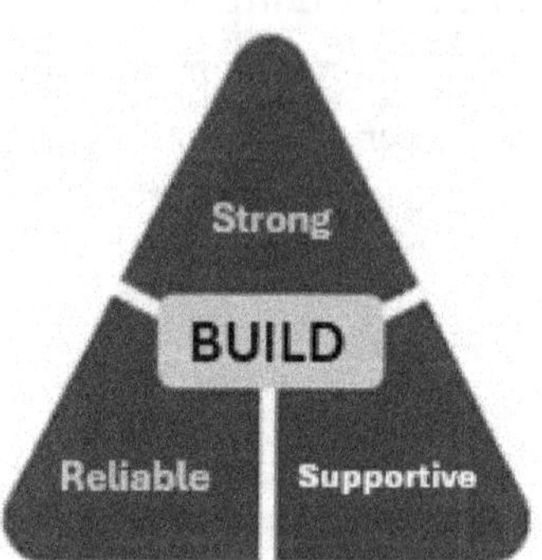
Strong
BUILD
Reliable
Supportive

Supportive

Being supportive within your business network isn't just a nice gesture—it's a strategic advantage that pays dividends in the long run. When you actively support others in your network, you contribute to a culture of reciprocity and goodwill. This can lead to strengthened relationships built on trust and mutual respect. Whether it's offering advice, making introductions, or simply providing encouragement, your support can make a significant impact on someone else's journey. In turn, they're more likely to remember your kindness and be inclined to support you when the opportunity arises.

Moreover, being supportive helps to foster a collaborative environment where everyone can thrive. In today's interconnected world, success often hinges on the ability to collaborate effectively. By lending a helping hand or sharing resources within your network, you contribute to collective growth and innovation. You never know how your assistance today might lead to a fruitful partnership or collaboration tomorrow.

Lastly, being supportive reflects positively on your own personal brand. It demonstrates that you're not just focused on your own success but also invested in the success of others. This can enhance your reputation as a team player and a leader who values collaboration. People are more likely to want to work with someone who is supportive and generous with their knowledge and resources. Ultimately, building a supportive business network isn't just about what you can gain—it's about creating a supportive ecosystem where everyone can thrive and achieve their goals together.

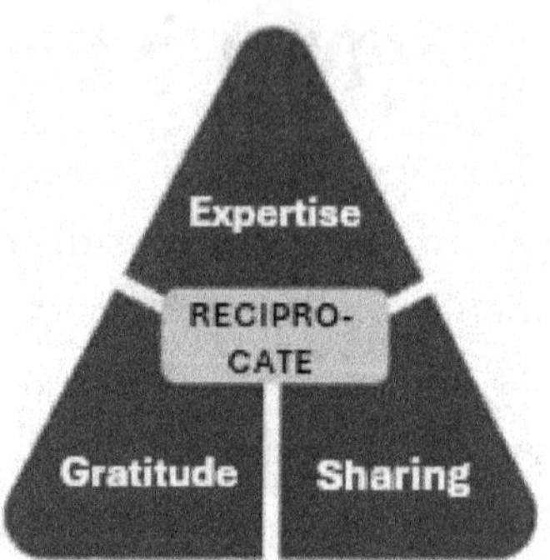

Expertise
RECIPRO-
CATE
Gratitude
Sharing

RECIPROCATE

Reciprocating with your network contacts is essential for building strong, mutually beneficial relationships that can propel your career or business forward. The first key to effective reciprocation is **expertise**. It's about giving freely within your network without expecting immediate returns. This could mean offering your expertise, making introductions to valuable contacts, or sharing resources and opportunities that align with their interests or needs. Generosity builds goodwill and trust, laying a solid foundation for future collaborations and support.

The second key is **gratitude**. Paying attention to the needs and challenges of your network contacts shows that you value their input and are invested in their success. This could involve actively listening during conversations, remembering key details about their goals or interests, and following up on previous discussions. By demonstrating gratitude, you signal that you are reliable and genuinely interested in fostering a meaningful relationship beyond superficial connections.

Lastly, **sharing** is crucial in reciprocating with your network contacts. Instead of waiting for others to ask for help or assistance, take the initiative to share opportunities when you can. This might include sharing relevant industry insights, recommending their services to others, or volunteering your time and expertise for their projects. Sharing shows initiative and a commitment to mutual success, strengthening your credibility and deepening your relationships within your network.

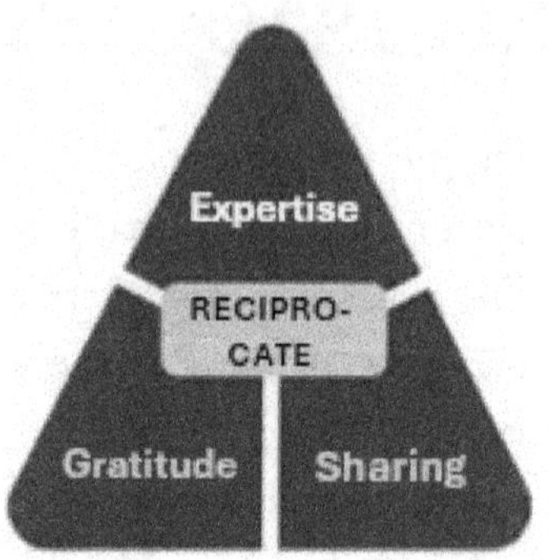

Expertise
RECIPRO-
CATE
Gratitude
Sharing

Expertise

Having expertise that others seek out can be immensely rewarding and advantageous in various ways. Firstly, being recognized as an expert in a particular field or skill brings credibility and respect within your professional community. When others come to you for advice or guidance, it affirms your knowledge and expertise, boosting your confidence and reputation. This recognition can open doors to new opportunities such as speaking engagements, collaborations, or leadership roles, enhancing your career prospects significantly.

Secondly, having expertise that others value fosters a sense of fulfillment and purpose. It feels gratifying to know that your skills and knowledge are making a meaningful impact on others' lives or businesses. Whether you're mentoring colleagues, consulting with clients, or sharing insights at industry events, the opportunity to contribute positively to others' success can be personally fulfilling. It strengthens your sense of professional identity and motivates you to continually improve and stay current in your field.

Thirdly, being the go-to expert can lead to expanded professional networks and valuable connections. People naturally gravitate towards experts when seeking advice or solutions, which can lead to new relationships and collaborations with like-minded professionals or organizations. Networking becomes easier and more fruitful when you're known for your expertise, as it facilitates introductions and opportunities for collaboration on projects or initiatives where your specialized knowledge is valued and sought after.

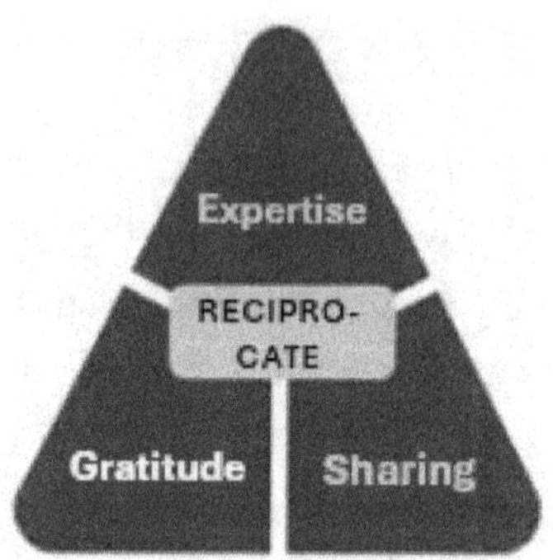
Expertise
RECIPRO-
CATE
Gratitude
Sharing

Gratitude

Expressing gratitude in your business career is not only courteous but also essential for building strong relationships and fostering goodwill. One effective way to show gratitude is through a heartfelt thank-you note or email. Taking the time to write a personalized message detailing how the person's assistance benefited you or your business demonstrates sincerity and appreciation. This small gesture can leave a lasting impression and strengthen your professional rapport with them.

Another way to express gratitude is through public acknowledgment and recognition. For instance, publicly thanking someone during a team meeting, in a company newsletter, or on social media can showcase their contributions and highlight their expertise to a broader audience. This not only boosts their morale but also reinforces a culture of appreciation within your workplace or professional network. Additionally, offering to provide a testimonial or endorsement for their services or expertise can be a meaningful way to reciprocate their support and showcase your appreciation.

Lastly, consider offering a token of appreciation or a small gift to express gratitude. This could range from a thoughtful gift related to their interests or profession to treating them to a meal or coffee. Gifts don't need to be extravagant; what matters most is the thought and effort put into selecting something meaningful to show your gratitude. These gestures not only convey your appreciation but also strengthen the personal connection between you and the individual who has helped you along your career journey.

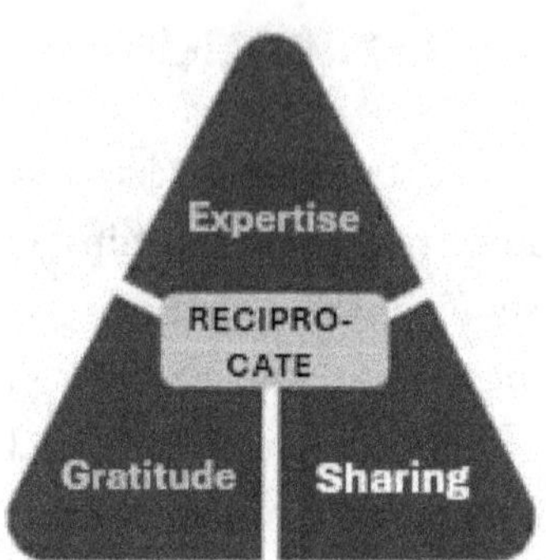

Expertise
RECIPRO-
CATE
Gratitude
Sharing

Sharing

Sharing business information with your network can yield numerous benefits, fostering a culture of collaboration and mutual support. Firstly, sharing insights and knowledge demonstrates generosity and goodwill, which can strengthen your relationships with peers, colleagues, and industry contacts. By openly sharing information such as market trends, industry news, or successful strategies, you position yourself as a valuable resource within your network. This can lead to reciprocity, where others are more inclined to share their insights and information with you in return, creating a more dynamic and informed community.

Secondly, sharing business information can enhance your reputation as a thought leader or expert in your field. When you consistently provide valuable information and perspectives, you build credibility and trust among your peers and within your industry. This can lead to increased visibility, opportunities for speaking engagements, media inquiries, or invitations to contribute to industry publications. As your reputation grows, so does your influence, allowing you to positively impact your network and potentially attract new business partnerships or clients who value your expertise.

Thirdly, sharing business information can spark innovation and collaboration. By exchanging ideas and perspectives with others in your network, you gain fresh insights and diverse viewpoints that can inspire creative solutions to challenges or opportunities. Collaborating on projects or initiatives based on shared information can lead to synergies where each party benefits from collective knowledge and resources. This collaborative approach not only accelerates growth and innovation but also strengthens the bonds within your network, creating a supportive ecosystem where everyone can thrive.

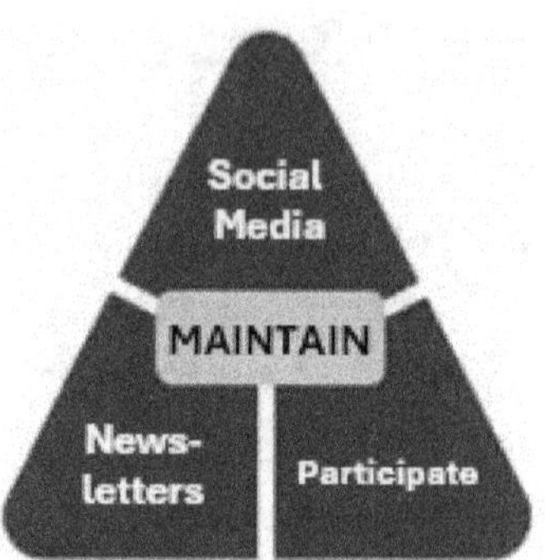
Social
Media
MAINTAIN
News-
letters
Participate

MAINTAIN

Maintaining your business network requires consistent effort and the use of effective tools to stay connected and engaged with your contacts. Firstly, leveraging **social media** platforms such as LinkedIn can be instrumental. Regularly updating your profile with relevant information about your professional achievements, sharing industry insights, and engaging with posts from your connections helps to keep you top-of-mind and reinforces your presence within your network. Additionally, LinkedIn's messaging feature allows for direct communication, making it easy to reach out to individuals for follow-ups or to share valuable resources and updates.

Secondly, email **newsletters** can serve as a powerful tool for nurturing your network. Sending periodic newsletters that provide industry news, company updates, or helpful tips demonstrates your expertise and keeps your contacts informed. Personalizing these newsletters by segmenting your contacts based on their interests or preferences can enhance engagement and relevance. Including a call-to-action encourages recipients to reach out or respond, fostering two-way communication and strengthening your relationships over time.

Thirdly, **attending** and participating in industry events, conferences, and networking gatherings remains invaluable. These occasions provide opportunities to meet new contacts, reconnect with existing ones, and deepen relationships face-to-face. Before attending events, research potential attendees and set specific networking goals to maximize your time and interactions. Following up after events with personalized messages or invitations for further discussion helps to solidify connections made and sustain momentum beyond the initial meeting.

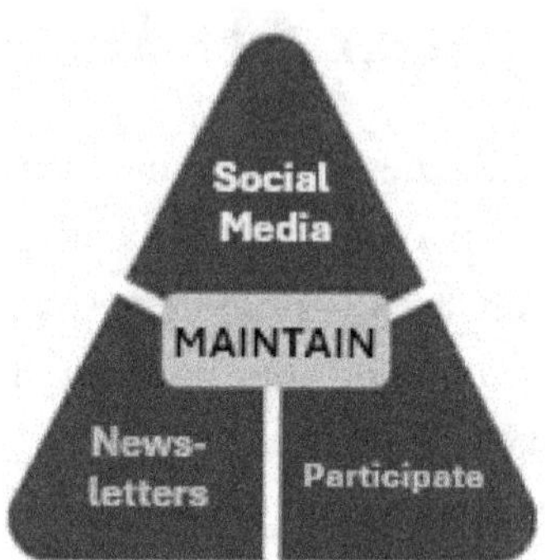
Social
Media
MAINTAIN
News-
letters
Participate

Social Media

Social media has transformed business networking by providing a powerful platform for connecting with professionals globally. One of its key advantages is accessibility—it allows you to reach a vast audience of potential collaborators, clients, and industry influencers with just a few clicks. Platforms like LinkedIn, Twitter, and Facebook offer dedicated spaces for sharing your expertise, showcasing your achievements, and engaging in conversations that can expand your network exponentially. Whether you're a seasoned entrepreneur or just starting out, social media levels the playing field, offering opportunities to network and build relationships regardless of geographical boundaries.

Moreover, social media facilitates real-time interaction and engagement. Through comments, likes, shares, and direct messages, you can initiate conversations, seek advice, and share valuable insights with your network instantaneously. This immediacy not only strengthens existing connections but also allows you to discover and connect with new contacts who share similar interests or goals. Engaging actively on social media shows your commitment to staying informed and involved in your industry, positioning you as a proactive and valuable member of your professional community.

Additionally, social media provides invaluable tools for personal branding. By curating your profile and sharing content that reflects your expertise and interests, you can shape how others perceive you professionally. Consistently posting relevant updates, articles, and success stories helps to establish credibility and build trust among your peers and potential business partners. Furthermore, participating in industry-specific groups and forums on platforms like LinkedIn allows you to join conversations, exchange ideas, and contribute to discussions that can enhance your visibility and reputation within your field.

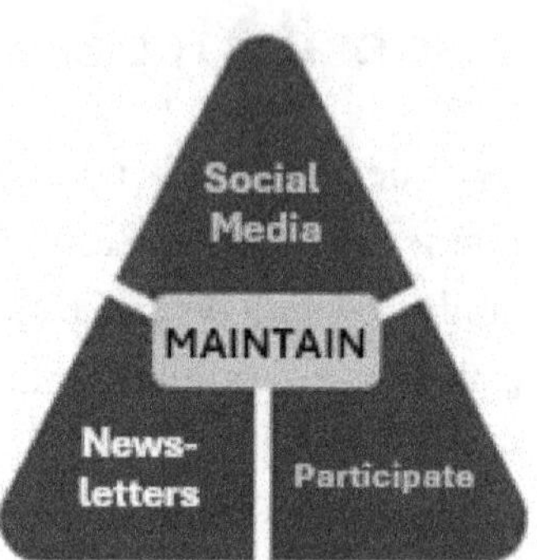

Social
Media
MAINTAIN
News-
letters
Participate

Newsletters

Sending newsletters on a regular basis to your business network is a practical and effective way to stay connected, informed, and engaged with your contacts. Firstly, newsletters provide a structured format for sharing valuable content such as industry news, company updates, and relevant insights. By curating and delivering this information directly to your network's inbox, you establish yourself as a knowledgeable source in your field and demonstrate your commitment to keeping your contacts informed and engaged. This consistency helps to strengthen relationships over time, fostering trust and credibility among your audience.

Secondly, newsletters serve as a powerful tool for maintaining top-of-mind awareness. By regularly appearing in your contacts' inboxes with relevant and useful content, you reinforce your presence and visibility within your network. This can be particularly beneficial when recipients are considering referrals, collaborations, or business opportunities, as they are more likely to think of you first due to the ongoing communication and value you provide through your newsletters.

Thirdly, newsletters enable two-way communication and interaction. Including calls-to-action such as invitations to connect on social media, RSVP for upcoming events, or provide feedback encourages recipients to engage with your content and take further steps to interact with you. This engagement not only strengthens the relationship but also provides valuable insights into the interests and preferences of your network, allowing you to tailor future newsletters and communications more effectively.

Social
Media
MAINTAIN
News-
letters
Participate

Participate

Participating in industry events with your business network offers numerous benefits that can significantly enhance your professional growth and opportunities. Firstly, these events provide invaluable networking opportunities. Meeting face-to-face with industry peers, potential clients, and collaborators allows you to establish personal connections that are often more memorable and impactful than digital interactions alone. Building relationships in person fosters trust and facilitates deeper discussions that can lead to future partnerships or business opportunities.

Secondly, industry events offer a platform for learning and staying updated on trends and developments within your field. Attending keynote speeches, panel discussions, and workshops provides access to the latest insights, best practices, and innovative ideas from industry leaders and experts. This knowledge not only keeps you informed but also positions you as a knowledgeable and well-informed professional within your network. Sharing these insights with your contacts further enhances your value as a resource and strengthens your relationships.

Thirdly, participating in industry events can enhance your visibility and credibility. Speaking at conferences or participating in panel discussions allows you to showcase your expertise and thought leadership to a wider audience. This exposure can lead to increased recognition within your industry, invitations for further speaking engagements, media inquiries, or opportunities to contribute articles or insights to industry publications. Your active involvement in industry events demonstrates your commitment to professional development and staying at the forefront of your field, which can positively impact your career trajectory and open doors to new professional opportunities.

Strong
BUILD
Reliable
Supportive
Expertise
NET-
WORKING
Social
Media
RECIPRO-
CATE
MAINTAIN
Gratitude
Sharing
News-
letters
Participate

SUMMARY

As you may have heard me say before "It takes years to build credibility and one day to ruin it." Networking is what solidifies your career and makes you a respected asset to your business community.

If someone chooses not to network in business, they may miss out on valuable opportunities for growth, collaboration, and professional advancement. Networking is not just about making connections; it's about building relationships that can lead to new clients, partnerships, career opportunities, and industry insights. Without a network, individuals may find themselves isolated from industry trends, developments, and potential mentors or peers who could offer guidance and support.

Moreover, networking plays a crucial role in personal and professional development. By engaging with others in your field, you gain access to diverse perspectives, new ideas, and knowledge that can broaden your understanding and help you stay competitive. Networking also enhances visibility within your industry, which can be essential for career progression or business success. Without an active network, individuals may struggle to stay informed about market changes, miss opportunities for professional growth, and find it challenging to navigate career transitions or business challenges effectively. Ultimately, while networking requires time and effort, the benefits of building and maintaining relationships in business are often indispensable for long-term success and fulfillment in your career.

Invitation

The last time I counted, I had over 3,000 contacts in my Rolodex (an old term) from a 50+ year career in Oil and Gas sales. I made over 35,000 sales calls (averaging five sales calls per day, five days per week, not including holidays) and drove over 700,000 miles (averaging 24,000 miles per year).

When I decided to work as a self-employed consultant, I would visit various manufacturers and distributors in the O&G industry to consult for them. During the interviews it would go something like this: "Well Don, your reputation precedes you. Seems like everybody in the industry knows you. Tell me, who are some of the contacts you have out there that you could take us to?" At that time, I would pull out my contact lists that I had typed out and lay them on their desk. After looking at it, they would usually say something like "Holy cow! This is impressive! When can you start working with us?!"

This is called "leverage." Your network that you've built over time will give you leverage and allow you the privilege to negotiate. If you don't have a network list built, then you have to take whatever others are willing to offer you and it's usually not very robust.

My invitation to you is that you take building a network seriously. The power of this will carry you all the way to retirement. It doesn't have to be in sales. It can be in any industry such as nursing, engineering, teaching, welding and so on. It is often said "It's not so much WHAT you know as it is WHO you know that helps your career." With social media, newsletters and participating in trade events, you should be able to get a good list going soon enough.

Here's a list of networking places where businesspeople can build their network:

1. **LinkedIn**: This is the go-to social media platform for professional networking. Salespeople can connect with prospects, industry peers, and thought leaders.
2. **Industry Events and Conferences**: Attend relevant conferences, trade shows, and seminars where industry professionals gather. These events provide excellent networking opportunities.
3. **Local Business Networking Groups**: Many cities have business networking groups where professionals from various industries meet regularly to exchange contacts and referrals.
4. **Chamber of Commerce Events**: Chambers of Commerce often host networking events for local businesses. These can be great for building connections within the local business community.
5. **Professional Associations**: Join associations related to your industry or sales specialization. They often host events and provide platforms for networking with peers.
6. **Online Forums and Communities**: Participate in online forums and communities related to sales, business development, or your specific industry. Engage in discussions and share insights to build your network.
7. **Alumni Networks**: Leverage your college or university alumni network. Alumni often have strong ties and can provide valuable connections.
8. **Social Media Groups**: Facebook Groups, Reddit communities, and other social media platforms have

groups focused on sales and business. Join relevant groups to network with peers.

9. **Networking Apps**: Explore apps designed specifically for networking, such as Shapr or Meetup. These apps match professionals based on interests and goals.

10. **Customer Networking**: Leverage your existing customers for referrals and introductions to their networks. Building strong relationships with customers can lead to valuable connections.

11. **Cold Calling and Prospecting**: While traditional, cold calling can still lead to networking opportunities. Engage prospects in meaningful conversations and explore potential mutual benefits beyond the initial sale.

12. **Business Breakfasts and Lunches**: Networking over meals can be effective. Attend business breakfasts, lunches, or after-work networking events organized by local businesses or professional groups.

Remember, effective networking is not just about collecting contacts but about building meaningful relationships and providing value to others in your network.

Local Networking

Know your local area like the back of your hand.

National Networking

Connect nationally through the Chamber of Commerce network

Global Networking

Know your global marketing through Trade Shows and other venues.

When you're with someone who is sharing their struggles with you...just smile at him/her and give them one of these. He/she will ask "What is that?" Then simply reply "Life Works in Threes."

Other titles coming out:

- Weight Struggles?
- Abundance Struggles?
- Parenting Struggles?
- Life Struggles?
- Purpose Struggles?
- Happiness Struggles?
- Sales Struggles?
- Speaker Struggles?
- Time Struggles?
- Romance Struggles?
- Marriage Struggles?
- Divorce Struggles?
- Money Struggles?
- Career Struggles?
- Dating Struggles?
- Caretaker Struggles?
- Forgiveness Struggles?
- Grieving Struggles?
- Success Struggles?
- Golf Struggles?
- Workplace Struggles?
- Stress Struggles?
- Shame/Guilt Struggles?
- Addiction Struggles?

Quotes about Networking

Your network is your net worth." - Porter Gale

"Networking is marketing. Marketing yourself, your uniqueness, what you stand for." - Christine Comaford-Lynch

"The richest people in the world look for and build networks, everyone else looks for work." - Robert Kiyosaki

"In networking, there is no privacy. Your name, your business name, what you do, your services, your products, your reputation, your integrity are open for others to see, hear, and pass on." - Michael Williams

"Networking is more about farming than it is about hunting." - Ivan Misner

"It takes years to build credibility...
and one day to ruin it."
Guard your reputation with your
life.

Remember,

When you get right down to it,

Life is about making choices.

Every day, all day long, that's what we do.

- *We choose to get out of bed or not.*
- *We choose to clean up or not.*
- *We choose what to eat all day.*
- *We choose to exercise or not.*
- *We choose to go to work or not.*
- *We choose to do a good job or not.*
- *We choose to come home or not.*
- *We choose to watch TV or do something constructive.*
- *We choose to bed at a decent hour or not.*

And the next day...we start all over again.

What is the meaning of this? Get good at choosing.

Before you can get good at choosing though...you need to understand how life works in threes.

When someone is struggling with a particular area or two, chances are they are "out of balance" with how life works. How does life work? Life works in threes.

If you're interested in personal topics like life, health, money or business topics like sales, time management and public speaking...Life Works in Threes! can shed some light on creating success in those areas.

The definition of TRIUNE is a group of three things; united. Being three in one, such as - humans are *mental, physical* and *spiritual beings.* The word TRYUNE is a play of the word TRIUNE, encouraging all to "try" this concept and help eliminate struggling unnecessarily.

LifeWorksInThrees.com